THE WHITE HOUSE

REMEMBERED

VOLUME I

THE WHITE HOUSE REMEMBERED

VOLUME I

Recollections by Presidents

RICHARD M. NIXON

GERALD R. FORD

JIMMY CARTER

and

RONALD REAGAN

·

Compiled & Edited by

HUGH SIDEY

·

With engravings by

THE BUREAU OF

ENGRAVING & PRINTING

WHITE HOUSE HISTORICAL ASSOCIATION

in cooperation with

THORNWILLOW PRESS

2005

THE WHITE HOUSE HISTORICAL ASSOCIATION
is a non-profit organization, chartered on November 3, 1961, to
enhance understanding, appreciation, and enjoyment of the
Executive Mansion. Income from the sale of this book will be used to
publish other materials about the White House, as well as for the
acquisition of historical furnishings and other objects for the
Executive Mansion. Address inquiries WHHA, 740 Jackson Place,
Washington, D.C. 20006. www.whitehousehistory.org

This edition of the *White House Remembered* is reprinted from
the handmade, leather-bound volume, published in a
limited edition by Thornwillow Press, Ltd.

ISBN: 0-912308-94-X

Library of Congress Catalog Card Number: 2005023317

Printed in the United States of America

CONTENTS

ILLUSTRATIONS

FOREWORD

THIS IS THE FIRST VOLUME OF WHAT THE White House Historical Association hopes will be a continuing series of observations and fresh rememberances by presidents and first ladies of actual life in the White House: the big things and the small things, the great moments of state and the tiny details of daily existence. Our hope is to get interviews with the presidents and the first ladies after they have spent some years in the White House and have adjusted to its spaces and routines as home but before they are long gone and recall gets fuzzy. We seek the real stuff of history; not only the background and mechanics of White House events, but also the moods and feelings that settled on these extraordinary people once in the White House, and their views of the history of which they have become such an important part.

The incubation of this volume was long and sometimes uncertain, given the demands on the time of the presidents and first ladies. We include four presidents who were in one way or another able to spare us some time:

Richard Nixon, Gerald Ford, Jimmy Carter, and Ronald Reagan.

Two of them died during the years of compiling the book, which makes our record even more valuable. We can always go to the memos and news accounts of the events of each administration but we cannot after the fact gather the phrase or the chuckles from a president or first lady as they recall their days living in the most renowned house in the world.

The funerals of the two men who died reflected in a way the undiminished glory of living in the White House. Nixon was forced from office, disgraced in the eyes of critics, yet when the services were held for him in Yorba Linda, California, his birthplace, leaders from around the world came to show their respects. He had been in the sacred ranks of presidents. Ronald Reagan's farewell stretched across the country, from Washington to his resting place at his presidential library in Simi Valley, California.

Thousands upon thousands came to pass by his body lying in state in the U. S. Capitol and more thousands looked up in tribute from towns and cities as Air Force One bore him westward in a final salute. The child of the Great Depression, the movie actor turned politician who gained the White House had led the world while he lived there and history would remember.

HUGH SIDEY

Strange offspring, the white house: born of revolution, proportioned by grace, sustained by wealth and power. It is a symbol of hope for American people.

The White House could possibly be the most renowned building in the world today. Certainly there are more exotic edifices (the Taj Mahal), older residences (Buckingham Palace), and grander executive centers (the Kremlin), but the prominence of the United States in this century has made the White House one of the most famous symbols of freedom, recognized in homes not only across America, but also nations around the world. It is a backdrop for crucial deliberations and decisions in countless global crises. The North Portico, with its massive pillars, seems almost like a television set where legions of reporters stand as they explain the rush of events that bombard us, their hurried words broadcast to distant civilizations.

The White House, that grand matron, turned 200 years old on November 1, 2000. Two centuries ago, a grumpy John Adams took up residence not at all sure he wanted to live there. But the White House has never looked better than now. Here and there a practiced eye can pick out a tiny sag or wrinkle or the equivalent in building parlance. They are, however, footnotes to a rich history that enhance rather than detract from the beauty of the White House. The few smudges at the window corners from the fire of 1814 when the marauding British torched the place have been left as a show of quiet indignation. Chips from the bullets fired at the north facade from Pennsylvania Avenue in 1994 remain for detection by sharp-eyed visitors. Overall, however, the White House structure is stronger, its exteriors and interiors more polished, its electronic ganglia more sophisticated, and its climate more pure than ever before.

The White House sits in splendor on sunny days, a bright and busy island bordered by green within the massive gray, federal government. In the evenings it is bathed in golden floods and the chandeliers from within sparkle through tall windows. It is enough to make some want to come calling to sip a little julep and listen to "Stars and Stripes Forever" from the Marine Band in the foyer. It is part of America's heart and soul.

The White House is old by our standards and yet it is young. I can count nearly fifty years—a quarter of the total life of the White House of walking up the Northwest Drive in the constant pursuit of news, more of which is funneled through the White House than any other place. And like almost everyone who works in or around the White House for any time at all, I have come to view the building as an enduring and comforting friend in times of tragedy and as a counselor of caution in moments of national euphoria. It always whispers to me, "Nothing is as good as it may seem right now—and nothing is as bad as you may judge in the moment."

When I first came to Washington I became friends with Richard Strout, the *Christian Science Monitor* reporter who also wrote the column TRB for the *New Republic*. He had been on the beat since the presidency of Warren Harding, and he was a source of delightful reminiscence. I once asked him what moments, good or bad, stood out in his long career of covering the White House. Without hesitation he said his most memorable moment was during December 7,

1941, the night following the bombing of Pearl Harbor. As they had done historically in times of devastation, Washington residents and government workers began to gather on the residence lawn. In those days the gates were open to the public. Strout said it seemed as if there was some invisible force propelling them. Searching for some reassurance, for some sign of confidence, they shuffled along Pennsylvania Avenue and stopped before the North Portico in the cold night. Franklin Roosevelt appeared and said a few words to show his resolve and faith in the United States, but after he went back inside, the crowd lingered. Someone started to sing "God Bless America" and soon hundreds of voices joined in. Strout looked up at the White House and though it was darkened for wartime, it seemed to always be a symbol that could be trusted to sooth and bolster a shaken nation. The strains of the song echoed off the White House walls. The people then turned, went home, and began the job of winning the war.

I think it must have always been that way even in the days when they were building the White House. Democracy is not an easy undertaking. It is nurtured by turmoil and even, as Thomas Jefferson said, some patriot blood now and then. Just born, the squabbling young nation did not know where to build the President's House. Thank goodness for George Washington, who was not the most sophisticated American but certainly the most resolute. When he declared he wanted the federal government situated along the Potomac—the river of his chosen residence—no one could argue otherwise. There were whispers that real estate speculators were involved in the decision to site the White House in a swamp, and there may have been some truth to that. But George Washington, the father of the country, had a firm jaw and held to his choice. Even someone who has endured the indignities of modern construction could hardly imagine the difficulty of the eight-year construction.

There were foremen who argued among themselves and workmen who refused to work. When a house of ill repute sprang up among the shacks of the lonely construction crews, the sanctimonious Commissioners of the District of Columbia ordered it shut down, only to ignore the order when workmen protested.

Through it all, George Washington prowled the construction site and literally forced reluctant carpenters and stone carvers to finish the job. He was the founding father in more ways than one. He wanted Washington, as city and government, to justify his faith in the new republic, the one he had fought for. He made it happen. Sadly, he died only about a year before the White House was ready to be occupied.

According to William Seale, the preeminent White House scholar, the new White House was unrivaled in its stonework, and because of its size and purpose, it instantly became the most prominent building in every mind of the new nation's people. The porous, grayish Aquia sandstone, which had been quarried in Virginia and used for the mansion walls, was sealed with a special whitewash formulated by the Scottish stonemasons. "So grandly did it rise over the nascent city, so supremely complete did it seem compared with the Capitol, which was long yet to be finished," wrote Seale, "that it was the prize statement that Washington the city would prevail. The President's House dazzled the eye with the coat of whitewash the Scotsmen had brushed over the stone walls. It seemed less of stone than one monolithic, bright stone itself. Very early, perhaps even before John Adams moved in, but certainly within two years of his arrival, it gained its sobriquet, the White House."

The struggle to make the house truly habitable and fully furnished began. It was still incomplete when Thomas Jefferson turned it over to James Madison in 1809. Shortly after, British Admiral George Cockburn and Major General Robert Ross, with 150 sailors behind them, set both the Capitol and the White House on fire. A raging storm smothered the fire after the building was gutted. More than half of the stone walls remained in place and were usable, and in three years the White House was again a functioning home and office.

For years, few administrations passed without the White House at the center of political or physical turmoil. It stood on the northern rim of the Confederacy as an insult to the South. It was the home of Abraham Lincoln, reviled and beloved. In a sense, Robert E. Lee besieged the place in his four years of brilliant but failing generalship. Washington was always the target, the

White House the bull's-eye, and its brooding occupant the man to humiliate and depose. Lincoln's assassination thrust the residence into worldly legend beyond anything known before. It became the stuff of history texts and literature—and of myth. It became a temple in which dwelled the ghost of this godly figure.

One wit suggested it was a relief that Theodore Roosevelt did not win another term in 1912 because the then-aging building would never have survived the continued assault from his four rambunctious children, often led on indoor charges by the president himself, fifty-four going on twelve. The White House by then had acquired substantial years. Even though many renovations and face-lifts gave it a certain charm, the structure was clearly falling from all beams, which had been sawed and shifted. When workmen lifted Margaret Truman's grand piano up to the private quarters, one of the legs punched through the floor and underlying ceiling. President Truman, who considered himself an amateur architect, soon concluded the place was unsafe and managed to get $5 million from Congress for renovation. He moved across the street into Blair House, and the old mansion was gutted once again. This time, however, benevolent engineers and craftsmen strengthened the building with steel and concrete.

Technology has altered the White House workings, also giving a new shape to the presidential patterns of travel and political involvement. Nothing, however, had close to the impact of television. The White House became a stage for the president, his aides and his family while the presidency became a national soap opera with a daily episode. The drama was played out among the 132 White House rooms, at Camp David, aboard Air Force One, in the Rose Garden, and on the South Lawn. Every person who entered the presidential sphere was fair game for inclusion in the continuing saga—friends, parents, children, cats, dogs, and goldfish. When the elm tree planted nearly 160 years ago by John Quincy Adams died in 1990 from Dutch Elm disease, it was worth a moment of mourning on the nightly news. When a drunken pilot of a private plane three years later unsuccessfully tried to crash into the White House, the fact that he sheared a branch off a magnolia tree planted by Andrew Jackson was worthy of television commentary.

Almost from its inception, the White House was a coveted subject of revision by architects, engineers, politicians, and even plain dreamers. While Washington and the government expanded dramatically to match the strength and purpose of the nation, the White House stayed remarkably intact however. Its original structure was supplemented only with modest office wings and its grounds were kept to 18.3 acres.

But there have been a considerable number of meddlers, including Caroline Harrison, the wife of Benjamin Harrison, who would have made the White House into a massive and garish complex if she had had her way. Architect Paul Petz proposed a huge hilltop palace resembling Versailles in France. To celebrate its centennial in 1900, U.S. Army Engineers planned gigantic round wings at either end of the existing mansion, giving the building the aura of an open house. All the plans fell of their own bad taste or perhaps even from the fact that the stately but simple lines of the White House had simply taken root in the American soul. It would not be changed.

Theodore Roosevelt added a low and unintrusive complex of offices to the west in 1902, and his cousin Franklin did the same thing to the east in 1940, but the proud lady in the middle ruled as before.

I first came under the spell of the White House in 1957, during Dwight Eisenhower's second term. I was excited on that first visit, but that was of course expected. I walked up the driveway with a quickening pulse, noting the black limousines that slid in and out of the gate and the faces passing by like that of Secretary of State John Foster Dulles, heretofore only a newspaper image. The building was not as imposing as I had thought, but it was like a centrifuge, ingesting people and information, throwing off decisions and proposals, and dispatching emissaries and task forces. It never seemed to quiet.

I can remember, as if it were today, hovering on the White House lawn to catch the fragments of news during the Suez and U-2 crises. I can remember when the old *Life* Magazine resurrected an original Mathew Brady camera and persuaded Ike to sit for a wet-plate picture in the Rose Garden. I watched and thought "how natural." I'm sure the old building remembers as well. The first photograph of it was a daguerreotype taken in 1846 or so by John Plumbe Jr.

After all the festivities the night after John Kennedy's inauguration, two reporters followed him back to the White House well after midnight. He stood on the North Portico, the snow from the night before piled high along the drive. He pulled on a small cigar and looked outward at the city still frenzied from the day's celebration and parade. The cold wind whipped his long tails. He was the picture of youth and exuberance, folded in the gigantic pillars of the White House. It could only be a good omen, I remember thinking, to see such a steady platform for an untried president.

I also remember standing on the porch outside the Oval Office when the Cuban Missile Crisis of 1962 had been resolved. With a wave, Kennedy headed to his helicopter for a weekend in the Virginia countryside. The sun shone on the White House and its warmth crept in. It was just another story for the history of this sturdy building.

The morning of November 23, 1963, I wandered on the front lawn of the White House as I waited for the body of Kennedy to arrive. Death was no stranger to that house, and I leaned against one of the old elms that lined the drive. I tried to count how many times a president had been brought down by the angers rampant in a free society. I looked at the softly glowing walls of the White House and again I felt reassurance.

The Vietnam protesters came in Lyndon Johnson's time, and they filled the night with their chants and lighted candles. Johnson closed the drapes on the north side of the White House to dampen the sound and fury. The White House was a redoubt inside, and yet it was still a symbol of understanding and hope for those who watched from the outside.

When Jimmy Carter signed the Camp David Peace Accords on the North Lawn with the bells of St. John's Church pealing from across the street, the old mansion smiled down in a new coat of paint, surrounded by grass—the bright green of spring. It was a happy time. And I leaned again on an elm and remembered how it had been on the night of Kennedy's death and how the White House had spoken to me that tragedy passes, as all things do. Maybe, I thought, the building was murmuring to me now not to let happiness carry me too far. She is a steady, sensible matron, that White House.

It is a curious fact of our lives, that the older the White House gets, the more it looks as it was intended to look at its inception. The colors, the graceful furnishings, the conveniences, the works of art, which none of those early presidents were able to assemble entirely, are now collected. The building glows under the touch of ninety-three people devoted to its eminence and place in American history. The good taste and acquisitions of Thomas Jefferson, James Madison, and James Monroe were broken up, ignored or, bent out of shape over the ensuing years, though Jackie Kennedy put the White House back the way it was intended to be. She succeeded beyond even her dreams and now the White House, while still a working office, is the repository of great treasures of furniture and art. Its authenticity is guarded by expert citizen committees, its structure is protected, and its profile is secure as long as the republic lives.

Even the modern security concerns have conspired in an unwitting way to return the White House to the original blueprints. The random shootings by disturbed people along Pennsylvania Avenue have prompted the closing of that section of the Avenue. Pierre Charles L'Enfant, who was hired by George Washington to lay out the capital city, never drew in a commercial street directly in front of the White House. He planned an expansive President's Park that included the White House grounds, what is now Lafayette Park, and the Ellipse. We may soon see such a pleasing prospect for the White House. Justly so for its third century of life.

RICHARD NIXON

RICHARD M. NIXON

THE FIRST TIME I SAW THE WHITE HOUSE was during the summer of 1936. I just drove by it: the event was nothing special. I was just a law student then and I was with a friend, but we went to Speaker Sam Rayburn's office and asked if we could watch a House session. We also asked for his autograph, but his secretary proceeded to sign Rayburn's name herself and give it to me. That was my first lesson in autographs. As I remember, I found the House session very interesting. I remember John Steven McGroarty, a congressman from California. He seemed like a poet on the floor.

As for the White House, I did not have a tour, I just went by. I wasn't even remotely thinking of the possibility of being there. At that point, I thought being a justice of the peace was a big job, which is quite true.

* * *

When I came back to Washington as a congressman for the first time, I saw the White House differently. I visited it on two occasions.

At one point, the Trumans had a White House reception for the members of Congress. Pat and I didn't really have all that much money, but she bought a new dress because we thought it would probably be the only time we'd see the place. I remember going through the reception line. Both Bess and Harry Truman were very gracious, but the aides had to keep pushing everyone through. I understood. The Congressmen and their wives numbered about one thousand, meaning the receiving would take two hours, even if it were hurried.

I remember the Trumans. Bess was very warm, reserved but warm, and he was quite down to earth. That wasn't the last time I saw him though. I was very fortunate for a freshman Congressman because I saw him again in the Oval Office in the same year, 1947. I had a very good friend on the Labor Committee, Charlie Kersten from Wisconsin. I also served on the committee, and in 1947, Kersten got the idea to call on some people; he was very interested in communist activities and felt we ought to call on some of the Eastern European ambassadors. He certainly had a lot of nerve. We got in to see the

Hungarian and Polish ambassadors, and this was at a time when almost no one got to see them. It has never been said but getting to see them was something. That's the first time I saw the face of communism abroad.

I also got to meet the president later. It so happened that both Kersten and I voted for the Greek/Turkish Aid Bill. It was the first major vote we cast in the Congress in 1947. The liberals in his Democratic district were against any military foreign aid and the conservatives in my Republican district were against any foreign aid, military or economic, so we both voted for it.

One day, Charlie Kersten came in and told me we got an appointment to see the president, so we went down and met him. All that I remember about it was that he was gracious. We were there perhaps only five or ten minutes, but he took us over to a globe, turned to the European area, and pointed it out. He was trying to tell us what the world was like, in effect. Looking back, I see what a remarkable thing the event was. We were two freshman congressmen, Republicans, and the president of the United States agreed to see us. Back then we thought that it was perhaps natural for him to do that sort of thing, but looking back, I wonder if I would have done it. It shows that he was working the Republicans though, probably because they had a majority in Congress. Anyway, that was the first time I saw the inside of the Oval Office, my first experience of it.

*   *   *

Having the White House as both a residence and an office may not make sense to some people. It may not make sense in terms of operating the office, but on the other hand, it isn't going to change and I don't think it should change. In the United States, we tend to become obsessed with the new and improved, but it's very important for us to be reminded of our roots. I wouldn't want to change the White House at this point. The only change I made was relocating the White House press corps to where the swimming pool used to be.

One Sunday early on in my term, I was walking around the house. I remember the reporters used to come into their old office and sit around. Helen Thomas [UPI reporter] was alone there working that day and I said to her, "My God, don't you have any better place to work?" She responded that that was all they had, so I came back and I told [my chief of staff H.R.] Haldeman, "Let's get rid of the swimming pool." I had used it a couple of times and Moynihan had used it, but it ended up being a great change to get rid of it. And the reporters all liked the change even though there were a lot of complaints at the same time. The critics thought we were destroying historical matter, but I was simply restoring it to what it was; I happen to be a conservative in that respect. I like conservative architecture as opposed to modern architecture and I don't take to modern art. As far as the White House is concerned, I want to keep it as intact as possible.

The German Chancellor, Kurt Georg Kiesinger, really brought that home to me. He was there for only a short time as one of our state visitors, and I remember taking him on a personal tour of the Second Floor of the White House. I took him into the Lincoln Sitting Room, where I worked, and to the Lincoln Bedroom, which, of course, was the Cabinet Room in those days. I also took him across the hall where Winston Churchill had stayed. When Churchill was spending the night at one point, Franklin Roosevelt put him in the Lincoln Bedroom because he thought he'd appreciate such an historic room. However, it is the hardest bed in the White House, so late at night, one of the ushers saw him in his nightshirt carrying his bag across to the Queens' Bedroom across the hall. It has a much nicer bed.

I showed Kiesinger all of this and he said, "You know, it must give you a great deal of pleasure and also inspiration, to walk in these same rooms that great men in the past have walked through. We don't have that in Germany anymore." I never forgot what Kiesinger said. That's the flavor of the White House, and that's what I want to keep.

* * *

I was never one of those that thought living in the White House was a burden, but I think it's very important to move around. I liked going to Camp David and Florida and I liked going to the Key Biscayne White House and the San Clemente White House, Casa Pacifica. I like to move from office to office even though the White

House itself I found very useful.

Incidentally, I'm unusual in one respect. I never used the Oval Office for creative work. Never. I signed things, or I'd have a meeting, a ceremony, or a discussion of schedules there. I found that as far as sitting down and doing the kind of work I do in writing a book and so forth, I used the EOB or the Lincoln Sitting Room. I prefer to work in smaller rooms.

The Lincoln Sitting Room is so beautiful that we recreated it in the construction of my California library. In Lincoln's time, it was the so-called Telegraph Room. Nikolay and Hay used to sit there, right outside Lincoln's office. I picked up a lot of history about the White House from the old hands who worked there, like Mr. Bruce [Prescott Bruce, the doorman]. He must have been sixty-five or seventy, and he used to reminisce and tell me all sorts of stories. I don't know how many of them were true, but he thought they were true, so I believed him.

The Lincoln Sitting Room is where we got the message from [Secretary of State] Henry Kissinger from [Chinese Premier] Chou En-lai about the opening to China. It was a message from a head of state through a head of state to a head of state: from him to me through the president of Pakistan. Sitting in that room gives one a good sense of history. It was a room for contemplation. The EOB I often used for work, but I got my best ideas in the Lincoln Sitting Room or at Camp David.

I didn't spend much time looking out windows in those early days, but I liked the White House grounds. We had a big dog then, and I used to walk it around the grounds. I learned about the trees and the flowers, like the famous Jackson magnolias.

Living in the White House at the time of the Vietnam protesters was a burden for the family. It didn't bother me as much because at least I could try to do something about it. But it was very difficult for the family, especially with the noise. They have demonstrations now outside the White House of hundreds of people, but we had them by the tens of thousands, in fact, we even had half a million on one occasion. One time I went down to the Mall at dawn, down to the

Lincoln Memorial and there were hundreds of thousands of marchers. In those days, there were big demonstrations and sometimes they could get rough.

In my White House years I did far more work at night than in the mornings, though I didn't get up too late, around 6:30 or 7:00 a.m. I never went to bed before midnight, however, and sometimes far beyond midnight. Those were long days, but I've changed over the years. I am now basically a morning man. I wake up at 5:00 a.m., go to bed at 11, and sometimes take naps.

Incidentally, I took naps in the White House too when I could, but I never went back to the residence for them as some did. I just went over to the EOB. I always took naps right there on the couch. It was quite useful. I remember Johnson was the one that put me up to it—he used to talk to me about his schedule of two days in one. He said, "I would come in in the morning, I'd do my work and so forth, and that would finish my first day. I would take my nap then come back. My second day would run from maybe 2:30 in the afternoon to 6:30 or 7:00 at night."

Now I go to bed at about 11:00 p.m. and get up at 5:00 to take a walk for half an hour. Creative work and writing I do from 7:00 to 11:00 a.m., those are the best four hours of the day. Raymond Moley taught me that. When he was seventy, he was still writing a column. I said, "How do you do it?" He said, "I know I'm getting older." He was one of the wonder boys during the early Roosevelt years. "I can't do as much as I used to, but for four hours a day I am better than I ever was. I have more experience." That's about my speed now. I work in the morning and see people in the afternoon.

* * *

I used to walk through the White House sometimes and look at the portraits of the other presidents. I liked them all because I liked history. I probably read more history and biography than most because in the evenings we never watched the news. I didn't like watching myself on television, so I just read instead, mostly in the Lincoln Sitting Room.

I don't read recent history. Unless history is fifty years old it isn't ready to read. It's like

Bordeaux; a good Bordeaux isn't good to drink until it's twenty years old. I prefer books on TR and Wilson, but there was also Jefferson and Jackson. Sometimes I could feel them there with me and I would remember what Kiesinger said. "It must be a great inspiration to you and a great comfort and pleasure to walk here in this place where great leaders of the past have walked, Lincoln, Jefferson, and Washington." Of course Washington never walked in the White House: he built it, but he didn't get to live in it. You really have to stop and think when you live in the White House. I once noted the place where Roosevelt's wheelchair went and I could feel that he had been there. It makes me reflect on all that he had done.

* * *

Ceremony in the White House is important, but it is more important for the visitor than the occupant of the office. Reagan once said, "When you've seen one redwood you've seen them all." I can say that when you've seen one State Dinner, you've seen them all. In fact, if you've seen one inauguration or convention, you've seen them all.

On the other hand, there is a good feeling in performing ceremonies.

I first got the feel for the importance of ceremonies when I was vice president. For eight years I attended all the State Dinners. We would always go up to the Yellow Oval Room in advance where Eisenhower had his swords and decorations magnificently decorating the room. There, we would mingle with the table guests— just the top half dozen or so—and at some point the Marine Guard would come. They would say, "Permission," asking permission to remove colors. Eisenhower, standing erect, would say, "Permission granted," so they could remove them. The ritual made a big impression on me. I did that as president, and it is still done because such ceremony is very important.

Truthfully, I never failed to get some inspiration out of these rites. Hearing "Hail to the Chief" or "The Star Spangled Banner" always picked me up. The colors and the pageantry must be done right though, low key. Either Kennedy or Johnson moved the greeting ceremonies from National Airport to the South Lawn, and now it is just beautiful.

During his term, Eisenhower never went to the airport, so I got to go. It was quite a privilege. I went to meet Churchill and rode to the White House with him. The government workers were given time off to go to the ceremony, but nobody came out to the airport—not even for Churchill. I rode in the motorcade with him back to the White House, and when I got back I told Pat that we had to do something about this: Churchill arrived and there were only a few scattered people there. My God, I thought, they turn out for a vice president but not a foreign head of state, like a current prime minister. Government workers are very blasé about state visitors and nothing was done about that during my time as vice president. One of the things I was glad to see had changed when I became president was that the ceremony then took place on the South Lawn with the red carpet.

De Gaulle was wonderful with ceremonies. When I took my first trip to France in 1969, they laid out a magnificent red carpet and did the splendid honor guard for me. I asked Dick Walters, who did our translating, about it. "Dick," I said, "that was really great. Does he do that for everybody or does de Gaulle do this just for top people?" Walter says, "No, he does it for everybody. He says he feels it is very important, particularly for the former French colonials. So whoever it is—it doesn't make any difference what former French colony comes in—they get the same great treatment because de Gaulle thinks it is a small price to pay for good relationships."

* * *

Watergate was a tough time in the White House, of course, but the toughest times were really the war decisions. The toughest one came one December, the decision which brought the Vietnamese to the table and allowed Henry Kissinger to negotiate the peace agreement in Paris in January 1973. Others were the Cambodian bombing and the China initiatives. Those were the sorts of things that brought us back to the Lincoln Sitting Room, where we generally would discuss these matters. Henry Kissinger made twelve secret trips on the Vietnam thing, and he usually reported back to me in that room. You can only seat three or four there, but as I said before, some way or another, it's the room where I felt we did the most organized and disciplined thinking.

I tended to compartmentalize. I either did business or ceremony, so living near the office never bothered me. We seldom discussed official matters at dinner, and we had some wonderful times. Christmas was outstanding because Pat did such a great job decorating. We would have done more in the second term if we'd survived because I had some ideas. The spring was incredible too with all the flowering apple and crab apple trees and the tulips. The White House grounds in springtime is one of the great sights of the world in my mind.

One of the best things we did—and something I found very useful in keeping in contact with people—was the church service. We were able to invite a lot of people who would not normally come to the White House. I do not believe that the house should be an elitist place, that it should only host people who are well dressed or famous, although so-called ordinary people like to see celebrities. It's very important that the White House belong to all the people, so for those worship services in the East Room, we invited people like the White House staff. I remember Mr. Bruce, who has since died. He was so proud of his son, who was studying to be a doctor up at Harvard Medical School. One time, we invited his son and his wife down. We would invite secretaries and stenographers and, of course, they could bring their kids. It was one place they could all be together.

* * *

One of the things I was most pleased with were the flowers in the White House. As you know, from the first day on we liked flowers, and they put fresh flowers out and changed them every day in every room.

It was harder for the family to live in the White House than it was for me. They were cooped up. It's hard to get out to walk or do anything like that. The beauty of Camp David is that it lets everyone get out. I remember Carter was going to get rid of it. I sent a personal message to him urging him not to and he ended up using it for his major diplomatic achievement. I talked to Reagan about that just a couple of weeks ago. He said it was just a lifesaver for him because he loved to ride his horse and do that sort of thing.

*   *   *

I did not oppose Truman when he put in the balcony. We used the Truman Balcony all the time. I had too many problems with Congress to care about a balcony. Things should be done to the White House for utilitarian purposes. You could put in air conditioning and that sort of thing, but you should retain the majesty, the history, the beauty of the house. I said to the staff the day we left, "We've seen the great houses of the world and this one is not one of the largest, but it is one in which we feel at home. The White House is not just a house."

GERALD R. FORD

MY FIRST TERM in the House of Representatives I was put on the Committee on Public Works. I was the junior member on the Republican side, so you can imagine how inconsequential I was. That was around 1948 or 1949 when Truman walked out of the White House, refusing to live there because of structural problems. A big controversy arose on whether the house should have been torn down entirely, including the walls, or only the inside, leaving the original walls. All of this was within the committee's jurisdiction.

At one point, Truman invited the committee down to the White House for a Saturday morning tour. In the East Room, one corner of the ceiling was eighteen inches down. He explained that as presidents came and went, they wanted to change various things. Many had a builder cut some of the uprights and eventually the ceiling just started to fall. As he showed us around, he pointed out that there wasn't a single closet in the White House, only cabinets. He recommended that we leave the walls but rebuild everything

47

inside, so we rebuilt the whole place inside the original walls. I periodically went down there to follow the building progress, which was my committee's responsibility. If you built the same thing today, it would probably cost almost $100 million, but then it only cost $5 million.

* * *

That was not my first experience with the White House, however. My senior year in high school in Grand Rapids, 1931, one of the motion picture houses, the Majestic Theater, put on a campaign to pick the most popular high school students from the seven schools of the city. I won that and went to Chicago to meet twenty-five or thirty other high school students from all over the Middle West who had also won.

We all took the train to Washington and visited the White House and Capitol Hill. That was my first real exposure to the city. I stopped in the House and Senate chambers, and they gave us a special tour of the White House, which certainly had some impact.

The next time I really got to see the place, besides a brief visit when I was in the Navy, was after I was elected to Congress in January 1949. I have to say that I was overwhelmed with the opportunity, the honor. I really was. I was thirty-five and very enthusiastic, and I had naive ideas of the way things are and how I could affect them. But I really was in awe.

*　*　*

Another time I saw the White House was shortly after Lyndon Johnson took office. He invited four or five couples over for dinner on a Saturday night, people like Lindy and Hale Boggs, who was the Democratic majority leader. He gave us a tour through the White House like Harry Truman did, showing us his bedroom, in which there were three television sets so he could watch the 6:30 news on each network simultaneously. That was something. He also took us through and showed us the johns. Because he was so tall and long-legged, he had them moved at an angle so he could have room to stretch out. When they were straight, they were uncomfortable for him, so all of them in the private quarters were changed.

49

* * *

I was in and out of the White House throughout my time in Congress, of course never thinking I would live there. My move there after the
momentous events of 1974 was an interesting
story. As many know, we lived in Alexandria, in a
house that we had built between 1954 and
1955. When Nixon resigned, we didn't want to
push him out immediately, so they ended up
rather leisurely moving out. The staff took some
time moving their things, so we lived in
Alexandria, our old home, for the week. All the
Secret Service and the press seemed to change
our little old Alexandria neighborhood. During
the week, we went to Chicago for the VFW
National Convention, where I announced the
amnesty program for Vietnam dissenters. When
we came back to Washington, the White House
was ready for us to move in. It was to be our
home for the rest of our days in the Capital.

We arrived out at Andrews Air Force Base
then flew by chopper onto the South Lawn.
Though we'd been in the White House for all
kinds of business and ceremonial events, this was
to be our first night sleeping there. Stepping in

for the first time was an unbelievable experience. Everything of ours had already arrived. Rex Scouten, then the chief usher, gave us a personal tour. It was not as calm at night as it was in Alexandria, but I never had any trouble sleeping. Betty made sure we wouldn't be in separate bedrooms, famously stating that after sleeping with me for so many years, she wasn't about to change then. So we brought our own double-headed twin beds.

As the days went by, we found the White House to be a very practical place to work and live. The private quarters were quite comfortable. We fixed up what had been a bedroom during Nixon's term to a sitting room, and I had some exercise equipment put in there. I'd get up in the morning and do my exercises there.

Our children, Susan and Steve, lived on the next floor up in some nice rooms. When Mike, his wife, and Jack came, they were taken care of, though I'm not sure where. We became very fond of the professional help at the White House.

Betty and I liked the Truman Balcony. We would go out there on a pleasant night for a wonderful panoramic view of Washington. From there, we could sit and watch the city and the monuments. The solarium, up on the third floor, was also very beautiful. You can actually get a better view of the city and the Potomac River Valley from there than you can from the Truman Balcony. It is truly a gorgeous view; we used to go up there and enjoy it with some drinks.

*　*　*

I had a little cubby hole office where I did much of my work. It was off to the left and down the hall from the regular president's office. I think that was a room that Haldeman had used for his personal office during Nixon's term. The Oval Office was too grand and luxurious for some of the mundane work, so I would go in the other room, often eating lunch there too.

I didn't have a spot outside where I worked, but I used the lawn a good deal for other things. I played a little tennis and occasionally I'd go out to hit a few golf balls on the putting green the golf organization put in. I also always enjoyed the Rose Garden even though I'm not an agriculturalist. Those gardeners did a magnificent job; it is very beautiful.

There was another room that I liked very much: the Map Room, which was on the right hand side of the exit hall to the South Lawn. That was the room where Betty and I met Dick and Pat the day they took off. From there, we escorted them up to the helicopter waiting on the South Lawn. It was a very moving and emotional time. What could I say to an old friend at a time like that?

Up in the private quarters, we spent a lot of time in the reading room, especially at night. I would take some work up, and Betty would watch television or do her work. And when we had personal guests we would have a drink with them there. The President's Dining Room is right off it, so that made it convenient.

* * *

I was always proud to have foreign leaders come to the White House. It is not as big as some of their homes, but it's got unique American charm. One time, I really realized how personal and business areas coincide there. During the Bicentennial celebration, we had many State Dinners for the heads of government. The biggest one, white tie, was held for Queen Elizabeth and Prince Philip. When the guests arrive for an occasion like this, the president and first lady go out to the front to meet them, escort them to the elevator, and take them to the Yellow Oval Room in the living quarters. We escorted the queen and prince to the elevator and when the door opened on the second floor, there was our son Jack standing with his pants on but his shirt off. And he says, "Oh, I'm trying to find my dress shirt and my studs." Betty apologized, but the queen said, "Don't worry, we have one just like it."

* * *

Living in the White House was a beautiful experience. All of it. Maybe one of my most moving memories is from late afternoons at the White House as the sun was going down and lights started coming on. In a way, it was an exciting time. I don't think I'll ever forget it.

As for the ghosts, we'd heard stories, but we never had any unusual experiences. Betty and I had Bob and Delores Hope in the White House several times. He was the principal entertainer and master of ceremonies when the Queen was there, so we had him stay over that weekend in the Lincoln Bedroom. He was convinced he had heard ghostly noises.

*   *   *

Not every hour in the White House was happy. The night we lost the election we had about twenty people over to watch the returns. We even had the television personality, Joe Garagiola, who had campaigned with us very hard for the last two or three weeks. Senator Jacob Javits and all of our children were also there upstairs in the private quarters. The early returns were not encouraging; we didn't win a state until Indiana. We started to pick up in the west but not enough. At about 2:30 a.m., [former governor of Texas] John Connally reported that it looked like we were going to lose Texas by 100,000 votes. It looked like the final blow so I went to bed. The next morning we had to issue a concession but I had lost my voice during the campaign, so Betty had to read it. I think if we'd had another couple of weeks, it might have turned around.

55

That last night in the White House was a sad time. We had Nelson and Happy Rockefeller and their two boys to stay with us overnight. The next day, we went up to Capitol Hill for the swearing in of President Carter, after which we walked down the back steps of the Capitol to get in the helicopter. I asked the pilot to fly over the White House, to see it for the last time before leaving. We certainly enjoyed living there, and we tried very hard to stay.

* * *

The White House was a good place to work and live. There were plenty of offices and while I was there I never heard any complaints. Maybe something needs to be done for the press corps, which seems to keep growing and growing, but I would never advocate that a president live some-place else and treat the White House as a muse-um. It ought to be inhabited by a family.

I am a strong advocate for the public to have access to the public parts of the building. Those people on tour never bothered me, and they were never around the Oval Office. I think there is ample room for everybody, and I don't see any need for great changes there.

* * *

Back when I became vice president, there was
a commotion about the vice president's residence. In 1960 or 1970, Congress passed
authorization for a vice president's residence, but
they never funded it. When Agnew came in they
had to install all the security at his house and
Congress got a little upset. Every time they had a
new vice president, they had to pay for an all new
security apparatus. When I became vice president, two of my friends in the Senate, Bob Griffin
of Michigan and Harry Byrd of Virginia, came up
with the idea of reserving the Admiral's House
for the vice president. I thought it was a good
idea, but I didn't want to get involved.

The two of them got Congress to authorize it.
It just happened that there was a vacancy in the
Chief of Naval Operations, and no admiral was
living in the house. If there had been an admiral
living there, I bet it never would have happened.
The navy was furious, but with all the other
things going on, they couldn't stop it.

At that point, we still lived over in Alexandria.
The General Services Administration came to
Betty and told her that changes were needed for

linens and china and so forth, so she was planning to go up to New York on a Monday with some government officials to pick out all these things. The Friday before, however, I got word from [White House Chief of Staff] Al Haig that the "smoking gun" tape from Watergate was going to come out over the weekend. "In effect," he said, "the odds are that you're going to become president in the next week."

That afternoon I went out to the Admiral's House with Betty. She wanted me to look around and see what it was like to help her make some plans for this trip to New York. I went out there knowing what Haig had told me, still going through the process with Betty. We went to dinner at the home of the *Washington Star* writer, Betty Beale and her husband, George. I didn't say a word, but back at our home after dinner I told her, "Betty, I think you better cancel your trip on Monday because I don't think we're ever going to live in the vice president's house." Well, she had to make excuses because it still was not certain that Nixon was going to resign. She cancelled her plans, and the press wanted to know what was happening, so we had to make some excuse. That was the first night we ever talked about living in the White House.

* * *

I've almost forgotten about the waffles. When we first moved into the White House, there was a story about me making waffles Sunday mornings, however, I didn't get into the kitchen much after the first few days. The help is great and they resent intrusion. Indeed, all the services at the White House are superb, but I think presidents need to use them judiciously. The service in the White House is necessary for a president to do the best job. They even had navy specialists who took care of your clothes when you traveled. Every day, they would pack and arrange everything.

In my daily routine, if I had a regular day, I'd get up at 5:30 or 6:00 a.m. I'd have a cup of coffee and read *The Washington Post*, *The New York Times*, and any classified information that came in overnight. Then I would shower and shave. I'd usually go to the Oval Office at 7:30, meet with [National Security Advisor] Brent Scowcroft at around 8:30, then Secretary of State Henry Kissinger and my chief of staff, Donald Rumsfeld or Dick Cheney. The rest of the day would be appointments. Maybe once a week I'd have a Cabinet or NSC meeting when I had to make a decision on something, like nuclear negotiations. They would usually run until 6:00 p.m. or so, then I'd take a swim and go up to the private quarters, taking with me an hour or two of papers to look over. That would be a normal, uneventful day when I didn't have a luncheon or a foreign guest coming in.

* * *

The White House is a good place for handling world crisis. Everything is right there, and you don't have to travel in the event of an emergency. One good example is the Mayaguez crisis. I was awakened at about 5:00 a.m. by my aide Brent Scowcroft telling me there were unconfirmed radio reports that an American merchant vessel had been seized by the Cambodian military. He said that as soon as we got any more or verified information he would let me know. "Why don't I plan to see you at the Oval Office at 7:30?" I said and went back to sleep. When Brent came into the office, he had verification, and we knew then that the ship had been seized. We set up a meeting of the National Security Council around 10:00 and ordered surveillance planes from one of our Philippine bases. Then we turned around the aircraft carrier task group that was on its way to Australia for some ceremonial occasion, so it could come back and be available if we had to use the planes. Later that day we had another NSC meeting, and we ordered Marines to move and get ready should they be needed. All of that was done from the Cabinet Room. I went down to the Situation Room several times, but it was only a few steps.

I had ordered that no boats be permitted to go from the *Mayaguez* to shore because I didn't want them to take Americans like they had in North Korea years earlier. All these orders were executed right on the spot from the White House.

I guess it was the second day when we were having a Cabinet meeting when a young naval officer walked in and whispered in the ear of [the Chief of Naval Operations] Admiral James Holloway. He then said, "Mr. President, we just got a report from a plane flying over the ship saying there is a boat going from the ship to land. The pilot says it looks like there are caucasian faces on the boat and he wants to know what he should do. Should he destroy the boat?" We talked about it quickly. There was no time. "Tell him not to sink the boat," I said. It turned out that there were Americans being taken to the land, and if we had destroyed the boat we would have killed them.

The complex of the Situation Room, Oval Office, and Cabinet Room functioned very smoothly. We got the message back to the pilot in time, and he was able to carry out his orders.

* * *

Speaking of Marines, you can't beat the Marine Band, which plays at the White House and other ceremonies. One time, they gathered for the Queen of England's visit. After dinner I asked her to dance, but while I was dancing with her, they played "The Lady is a Tramp." I kept silent. I don't think she knew what the piece was, or at least she didn't let on that she did!

* * *

The White House is a great place for a president to do his work and live a reasonable life. Every president and first lady have somewhat different tastes and do something a little different to the White House, but I wouldn't think of significantly changing it at all.

JIMMY CARTER

JIMMY CARTER

As I walked down Pennsylvania Avenue and watched the inaugural parade from the White House, I obviously had a feeling of awe and respect. I had never seen the White House except from the outside and when I met with President Ford after my election in the Oval Office.

On the way between the parade and the White House we were confronted with an array of TV cameras. Everybody wanted to talk to me. I had just finished my inaugural speech and walked down Pennsylvania Avenue when Jody Powell, the press secretary, said, "I'd like to urge this whole family not to stop and talk to the press because we'll never get away." And, I guess typically, my mother said, "Jody, you can go to hell. I'll speak to whomever I please." The first question was, "Miss Lillian, aren't you proud of your son?" I moved very close to hear my mama's complimentary response, and she said, "Which one?" It kind of brought me down to earth.

Even after only a short time, the White House became a home for my family. We enjoyed it with

Amy as a little child and our son Chip, whose first baby was born a month after we moved there. Our youngest son lived there too and went to college in Washington. It became a regular home for us.

It was fascinating to be surrounded by objects that belonged to previous presidents. From reading histories about their own family lives, we were able to imagine how they lived and how they were just human beings. Each one was blessed with tremendous national and international responsibility, but he still had a home and went through normal experiences, dreams and sufferings as an average citizen must. We became immersed in the details of their personal lives.

Right away, I had the caretakers, the curators of the White House, take us around to see mementos of former presidents: the little writing desk that Thomas Jefferson made and carried around on his horse, the furniture that Lincoln had used, and the Map Room where Roosevelt and Churchill planned the Second World War.

Whenever we had an exchange of conflicting ideas or views, which our family has always had at mealtimes, we would be sobered by the fact that we would always have a different president's china on the table. We would think of the lives of those who had used them: Adams and Jefferson, Lincoln, Jackson, and Wilson, and many others. It was a constant daily reminder that we were sharing with them the history of a great country.

Rosalynn and my daughter-in-law went over to enormous storehouses where furniture of former presidents is stored, and they were able to select a table, piece of art, vase, or chair that appealed to them and that had probably been used one hundred years or more before.

We enjoyed the seclusion of the White House. The first two floors were, however, open to visitors almost all the time, and on the way to the Oval Office each morning or afternoon, I could speak to a few visitors if I wished. I had a pleasant time. My family and I swam in the pool, jogged every afternoon around the South Lawn area, played tennis, and on bad days, we used the bowling alley that Truman had built.

My favorite room was the Treaty Room. It was a beautiful space with an enormous chandelier and a table where Lincoln and his Cabinet had met. Several treaties had even been signed there.

I did my private work in the office adjacent to where Rosalynn and I slept. Between the bedroom and my office there was a very large bathroom, and beyond that was the office where I wrote my speeches, did my homework, tied flies—I'm a fly fisher, and listened to Willie Nelson and classical music. We had a very nice fireplace in that room and Rosalynn and I would sit and watch television there. We believed in saving energy, so we had different wood-burning heaters that we tried out. There was one in that room and two in the Oval Office and Cabinet Room. It was very pleasant sitting there in front of the fire, reading and watching TV.

For the Truman Balcony, we imported six rocking chairs from Georgia. I would quite often meet up with my staff members and cabinet officers there, and sometimes foreign visitors would come up and spend an afternoon with us. Many times after a state banquet, we'd go up and talk while looking over the Washington Monument, the Jefferson Memorial, and the National Airport. It is a very enjoyable place.

I wouldn't advise changing the White House, making it bigger, or adding office space. I think it's adequate. The bureacracy in the Executive Office Building and the New Executive Office Building is constantly growing. That's the better place to expand, but the best thing, I believe, would be not to expand at all.

The White House works for the president as a living space and an office space. When I had a very crucial meeting with senior Washington advisers, private citizens who had been in previous Democratic administrations, or with a very few members of the Senate or House, I would hold it in the Map Room or upstairs in the residence.

There's also a dining room down on the State Floor adjacent to the main entrance. That's where presidents always ate until Kennedy. He created a private dining room upstairs, across the hall from the master bedroom. In that little dining area, I met twice a month with the Democratic congressional leaders from the House and Senate. At times I would have as many as one hundred members of the House come over to the East Room to give them a briefing on a particular aspect of foreign policy. I really enjoyed that. We used the White House very effectively, and when we had foreign visitors, the reception, the banquet, and the entertainment afterwards were always held inside the White House or on the grounds.

One of the most striking memories from my term is from when I signed the Camp David Accords. After six months of negotiations after Camp David, we finally had a treaty between Egypt and Israel. We signed it on the lawn of the North Entrance to the White House with an enormous crowd. That night we had a banquet and about 1,000 people attended from Egypt, Israel, and throughout the United States. An enormous tent was set up on the South Lawn, with wonderful entertainment inside.

Another very impressive ceremony was when the Pope [John Paul II] came. I welcomed him on the North Lawn, and then we held a very large cermony, mainly for American Catholic leaders, on the South Lawn.

Amy was the one who explored the passageways in the White House and tried the secret door that went from the second to the third floor. There's no way to tell the door is there until you push on the wall. We also always had reports from our visitors about ghosts. They would always have some comment about movements at night in the Lincoln Bedroom, but I never detected a thing.

*　*　*

My hero for this century is Harry Truman. Truman was a historian, perhaps the best-educated historian that's ever lived in the White House. I read some of his impressions of the building itself and of its previous occupants; it was interesting to see the bipartisan relationships. The Roosevelt Room next to the Oval Office, you know, is to commemorate both Theodore and Franklin Roosevelt.

On the exterior walls, we could still see some of the burn scars from the War of 1812, when Washington was attacked by the British in 1814. Such things—the physical evidence of change during the presidency—are flavorful parts of the White House. A lot of the White House furnishings from the Federalist period were selected by Jackie Kennedy, but the Governor's Mansion in Georgia, where we lived for four years, had a superb, perhaps even better collection. By the time we moved into the White House, we had already lived in a house with such a decorating scheme. It made us feel a little more comfortable.

* * *

When I was living at the White House, I got up quite early in the morning to go to the Oval Office and read the secretary of state's nightly report, the local newspapers, and my paperwork. I tried to deter visitors until 8:00 a.m. when Brzezinski brought in the daily CIA intelligence report.

One of the first things I did when I got to the White House was estimate how much reading I would really have to do every day. I minimized it as much as possible and gave my staff instructions to abbreviate both the number and length of pieces of information that came to my desk. Over a period of time they became quite efficient at that. My wife and I also took a speed reading course with about forty members of the White House staff. I became quite proficient at it. As a result, I rarely had any work to do of a routine nature after 5:00 p.m.

So at 5:00, I would go swimming, meet with Rosalynn to jog, or play tennis with Dr. [William M.] Lukash, my physician. Quite often I'd go out by the C&O Canal or on the South Lawn near the Interior Department to run.

Living in the White House was a pleasant time for my family, and I would say that in the evening we basically enjoyed ourselves. There were obviously many times when we would have a special event, like the visit of some foreign leader. If I was not very familiar with the leader, I would have a special briefing about him or her: a psychological profile, the history of the nation, and what any pertinent issues might be.

We also would often have evening entertainment events even though I wasn't always particularly fond of them. One of the first things I did that aroused a lot of furor in Washington was to stop the reciprocal visits of dignitaries. Before I became president, if we had, for example, the president of Mexico come to the White House, the following night there would be an enormous official banquet at the Mexican Embassy. The president was expected to attend and always did. I didn't do that from the very beginning, starting with visits of dignitaries from Mexico and Canada. In some way, they looked on it as an insult to them, but I perpetuated that policy from then on.

In spite of that, there were a lot of evening events, though I'd say that the best times for me were probably those with my family. We almost always ate supper together, talking about our experiences of the day and I'd get their impressions about what was going on among college-age kids.

I think springtime was my best season at the White House. I'm a sort of amateur horticulturist; I guess "silviculturist" is the right word. I liked trees, so I learned the variety of species and the origin of all the trees on the White House grounds, which are quite extensive. In fact, when I left the White House, the gift I received from the White House staff was a detailed illustrated map of the eighteen acres with every tree, its common and Latin name, and its origin. Spring is also a time of good weather and relative seclusion from excessive visitors on the grounds.

* * *

I have to say that we really looked forward to Friday evening. If we were free, we would go to Camp David, which was a wonderful escape. We fished off in the little stream down the hill called Hunting Creek, and there were bowling alleys, jogging trails, a nice swimming pool, and a sauna.

* * *

For my last three days in the White House, I did not go to sleep. I came back from Camp David on Sunday afternoon and the following two nights, I didn't go to bed at all. I stayed awake getting the hostages out of Iran and completing that mission. I just stayed in the Oval Office and negotiated with the people involved:

the American Bank, the Bank of England, and the Federal Reserve Board. I also had to negotiate with the banks that were trying to keep all of the interest earned from Iranian assets that I had appropriated. Those were my last few hours at the White House: obsessed with the freedom of the hostages.

Even before I left the platform of the inauguration, I learned that the hostages had cleared Iranian airspace. When I left, I was totally exhausted but exhilarated. Indeed, I was exuberant. I don't think there's ever been a time in my life when I was more happy or grateful.

* * *

Living in the White House, a president shares a common responsibility and heritage with incredible predecessors and that continuity is surprisingly intact. The things that are dealt with on a daily basis to a surprising degree have been concerns of many of my White House predecessors, certainly those of this century. I gained both reassurance and inspiration from the fact that a president is part of a continuum of national greatness, that he personifies the hopes, dreams, and achievements of a remarkable country.

RONALD REAGAN

RONALD REAGAN

I WAS AMAZED HOW COMFORTABLE IT WAS to live in the White House. Over the years, it has gone through a lot of rebuilding and changing, but it still works. I once had a book on the history of the White House and after I started reading it, I couldn't put it down. It was the history of the house itself and all the presidents who had come, changed it, and added their own touches.

One Sunday morning I was sitting upstairs alone and I finished the book. Even though I had been living there for several years, I remember putting it down and walking through every room of the White House as if I were seeing it for the first time. As I went, I remembered where certain rooms were changed and then changed back again, the different color schemes and the different uses. It was a new view of the White House, and I was absolutely fascinated.

I had been in the White House no more than a couple of times briefly in meetings before I moved there. To walk into that house and know it was going to be your residence was something. I can't describe the feeling of having just taken the oath of office, been sworn in as president, and stepping into the house. A president goes up into the residential area where he has never been before to see the rooms where he will sleep, eat and live. I don't think a president ever gets over that kind of experience.

* * *

One of the reasons the White House is so comfortable is the people who work there. Every president agrees they are just wonderful. I'm quite sure the building itself catches their fancy and touches their hearts because each one becomes a part of it. And so, as Nancy has often said, they make living there a lot different than living in your own home. One could have any sort of mechanical failure or practical need, and in five minutes help would be there.

* * *

I was always very interested in the history of the rooms. Two that especially fascinated me were the Lincoln Bedroom and the Lincoln Sitting Room, which had been the Cabinet Room in Lincoln's time. There was enough of the original structure and furniture remaining there to give one a feel for what it must have looked like. Back then, this part of the White House was not only the dwelling, but the executive office as well. The president's office was where the Yellow Oval Room is, now a comfortable living area. In the old days, the landing in front of that office was always filled with press, job seekers and other visitors. It is so peaceful and totally devoted to residential use now, it is sometimes hard to imagine what it was like.

* * *

I was told once that the Oval Office's relocation to the West Wing was prompted by Teddy Roosevelt's wife. They had six children, and one day the hustle and bustle of the office got to be too much, so she finally said to Teddy, "You're going to find some other place for your office if I'm going to raise six children in this house." He did just that. They built the West Wing where the Oval Office is now, and it is functioning just fine away from the living section. When a president is home, he is home, and when he is at the office, he is at the office.

I think that every president since Harry Truman must have given a prayer of thanks for what he did in refurbishing the White House. One of the major things he did was build a balcony out from the residence area. At the time, he was criticized severely for it, but one can stand there now and look out over the South Lawn for a beautiful view. In the warm summer weather, I'd go upstairs for lunch out on the balcony. I always liked that. When the door opened, a lot of security configurations were triggered, which I always watched from above. Looking down, doors would suddenly open and gentlemen would come and go. They kept watch on the people around the fences down on the lawn, which made it seem perfectly safe and private.

* * *

When we moved into the White House, Nancy went to the storehouses where White House furniture is stored and found some fine things, which made the big hall into a wonderfully warm place. We had Speaker Tip O'Neill and his wife for dinner one night, and as we were walking down that hall after cocktails in the Yellow Oval

Room, he said, "I've been in this building many times but not recently and this is really the way the White House should be. I feel I'd be at home in every room, in every corner."

*   *   *

There have always been stories of ghosts in the White House. I knew a couple who were staying in the Lincoln Bedroom for a few nights and one morning the lady said that she had awakened and seen a figure standing down at the foot of the bed, looking out the window. When that figure turned, she realized it looked exactly like Abraham Lincoln. He then turned and left the room.

Her husband just couldn't believe it. "Oh, you must have been dreaming," he said. Believe it or not, sometime later he was almost on his knees apologizing to his wife because he subsequently had awakened and seen a figure standing at the other end of the room. He too saw that figure turn and leave through the door.

Yes, I think there is a ghost up there. When I told this to some of the veteran staff at the White House, the first thing one of them said to me was:

"Oh, he's back again?" Lincoln is still in the White House. I never saw him or any other ghost, but many claim to have glimpsed him.

* * *

The little study up in the private quarters, the one next to the bedroom, was particularly nice. There was a desk and a TV in there, and I felt like I could just step in with only my casual attire and be as comfortable as I wanted. The schedule for the next day was always delivered to me the night before in that study.

The Oval Office was more formal and I used it for ceremonies and visitors. The little study is where I did much of my real work. I also had a little hideaway near the Oval Office that I used quite often. Many times I'd lunch there, and every Thursday I'd lunch there with the vice president.

There were a few times when the private quarters were used for official business. When we were getting ready to run the rescue mission for Grenada we had to keep that secret, so we had the leaders of both houses of Congress meet with

84

us in the Yellow Oval Room in the residence. We did that to protect our forces. It was far more private and quiet in that room, and it worked very well to protect us.

*   *   *

The White House was attractive from almost any angle, but coming in by helicopter from the sloping South Lawn was the most beautiful view. Every season had its special charm at the White House. Christmas there is especially spectacular. One year, a gigantic Christmas tree filled the Blue Room and another lit the residential floor. When the spring and summer comes, all the flowers and trees bloom below. I especially loved the Rose Garden and the Jacqueline Kennedy Garden near the East Wing.

*   *   *

I'd have to say that my favorite time of day when I lived in the White House was the evening, when the business day was over and I rested upstairs in my home. We had some exercise equipment put in one of the rooms upstairs, and every day when I came out of the office, my first step was to peel out of my business clothes and work out.

*   *   *

Camp David is a wonderful part of living at the White House. We went there on any weekend we could. One of the other president's wives told Nancy to go to Camp David to relieve the stress of the White House, which was good advice. We would helicopter up on Friday afternoon and then back down on Sunday. It was a regular-sized home with a large veranda, and there was a putting green and a trap there so one could shoot. It was a great break from the stresses of Washington.

We used to invite our staff members, some of whom had children, up to visit. Nancy and I then started something. We had access to a lot of golden oldie movies, which we thought were much better than current pictures. We'd show one of them every couple of weeks and if we didn't show one for a while, pretty soon someone would say, "Why don't we have another golden oldie?"

The portraits of all the other presidents were in the public part of the White House and I enjoyed walking through to look at them sometimes. I felt a certain kinship to them. I could look at them and wonder how they felt in hard times and why they had done some of things they did. Looking at those portraits reminded me that I was living a part of this country's history.